DRAW PLUS MATH

ENHANCE MATH LEARNING
THROUGH ART ACTIVITIES

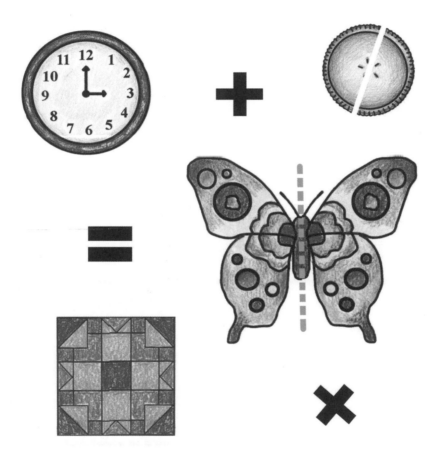

BY
FREDDIE LEVIN

Peel Productions Inc • Vancouver WA

Before you begin...

You will need:

- a pencil

- an eraser

- paper (recycle and re-use!)

- colored pencils for finished drawings

- a folder to keep your work

- a good light and a comfortable place to draw

Now, let's begin!

Distributed to the trade and art markets in North America by

NORTH LIGHT BOOKS,
an imprint of F&W Publications, Inc.
4700 East Galbraith Road
Cincinnati, OH 45236

(800) 289-0963

Published by Peel Productions, Inc.
Printed in China

Library of Congress Cataloging-in-Publication Data

Levin, Freddie.
    Draw plus math / by Freddie Levin.
        p. cm.
    Includes index.
    ISBN 0-939217-90-2 (trade paper)
    1. Art in mathematics education. 2. Mathematics--Study and teaching (Primary)--Activity programs. 3. Mathematics--Study and teaching (Preschool)--Activity programs. I. Title.
    QA19.A78L48 2010
    372.7--dc22
                        2010007724

Contents

Drawing Tips:

1 Draw lightly at first. **Sketch**, so you can easily erase extra lines later.

2 Practice, practice, practice!

3 Have fun with Draw Plus Math!

To Teachers and Parents

Welcome to **Draw Plus Math**! Children learn through all their senses. This book is designed to help your child or student enhance math learning through art activities with exercises and games that supplement math learning in a fun way.

The concepts presented include: numbers and counting, adding and subtracting, relative amount, sets or groups, one to one correspondence, shapes, symmetry, patterns, sorting, relative position, sequence, fractions, data analysis and graphs.

The lessons in Draw Plus Math are based on learning goals outlined by the Principles and Standards for School Mathematics, developed by the National Council of Teachers of Mathematics (NCTM). For more information, please access this website: http://standards.nctm.org

Basic Shapes

Basic shapes will be used in drawings. Practice these shapes.

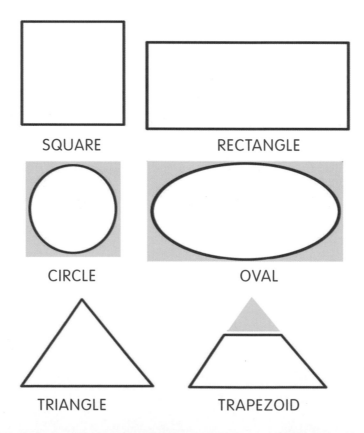

SQUARE   RECTANGLE

CIRCLE   OVAL

TRIANGLE   TRAPEZOID

Lesson One: I'm Counting on You

Look carefully at the fish tank. Answer the following questions by writing your answers on a blank sheet of paper.

How many **blue** fish are in the tank?

How many **purple** fish are in the tank?

How many **yellow** fish are in the tank?

How many fish have **stripes**?

How many fish have **dots**?

Can you think of another way to **count** the different fish in the tank?

How many fish are in the tank **all together**?

Let's draw some fish to put in a fish tank.

To make a round fish, start with an **oval**.

Draw a top fin, a bottom fin, and a tail.   Add an eye and lips.

Now, let's draw a thin fish. Start with a thin oval.

Add fins and a tail. Draw an eye and a mouth.

Draw the **rectangle** fish tank. Draw the **round** and **thin** fish you see. Make some with **stripes** and some with **dots**. Add the plants and rocks.

Color your fish tank picture.

Count the fish in your tank.
How many fish did you draw?
How many have **stripes** and how many have **dots**?
What other ways can you **count** the fish in your tank?
How many **thin** fish and how many **round** fish did you draw?

Fine fish!

Lesson Two: How Odd!

Even numbers end in **2 – 4 – 6 – 8** or **0**.
Odd numbers end in **1 – 3 – 5 – 7** or **9**.

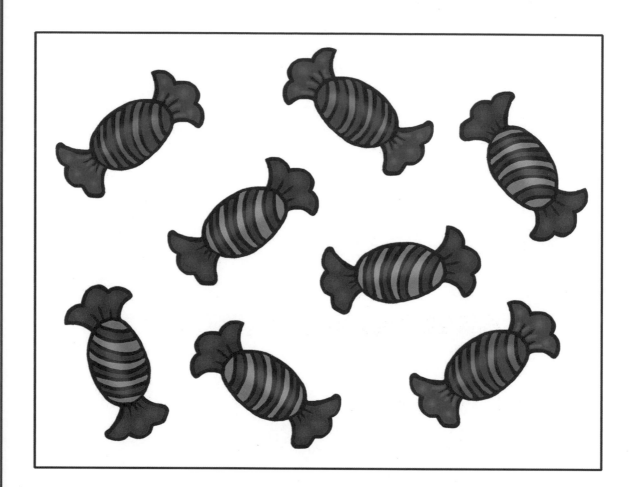

Look at the picture of candy.

Count the **red** candy. Is it an **odd** or **even** amount?

Count the **purple** candy. Is it an **odd** or **even** amount?

Count all the candy. Is it an **odd** or **even** amount?

Let's draw an **odd** creature.

Remember: **Odd** numbers end in **1 – 3 – 5 – 7 – 9**.

Start with **one** circle. Add **three** eyes. Draw **five** eye lashes on each eye.

Draw **seven** hairs. Add **one** nose and **one** mouth.

Draw a **triangle** body. Add **three** arms. Each arm has **three** fingers and **five** stripes. Add the fingers and stripes.

Draw **three** buttons.

Draw **five** legs. Add **five** wheels.

Color your **odd** creature.

Give it an **odd** name.

Crazy Creature!

Lesson Three: Let's Get Even

Even numbers end in **2 – 4 – 6 – 8** or **0**.

Count the party hats.

Is it an **odd** or **even** amount?

If you added one more hat,

would the amount be **odd** or **even**?

Let's draw a cake with an **even** amount of candles.

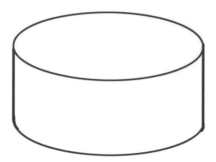

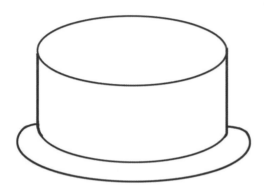

Start with an oval. Draw **two** straight lines for the sides of the cake and a curved line for the bottom.

Draw a plate for the cake to sit on.

Draw a candle with a flame. Add twisty stripes to the candle.

Draw **four** candles on the top of the cake.

Decorate your cake with flowers or whatever design you like.

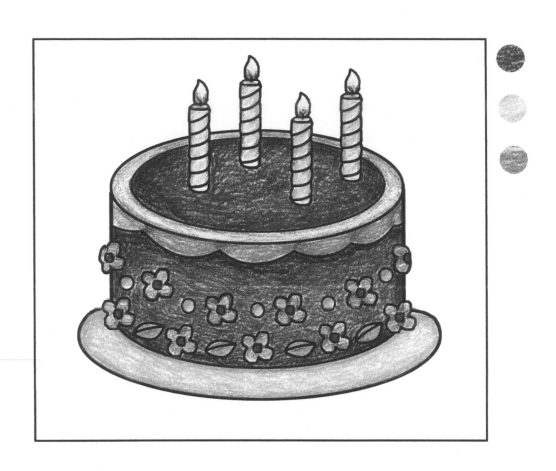

Color your cake.

How many candles did you draw?

Is it an **odd** or an **even** amount?

How old will you be on your next birthday?

Will it be an **odd** or an **even** number?

Lesson Four: One on One

Count the frogs.

Count the hats.

Each frog needs a hat. Are there enough hats?

Let's draw a frog.

Start with an oval for the eye. Draw a small circle inside the oval. Draw a curving line for the frog's head and back.

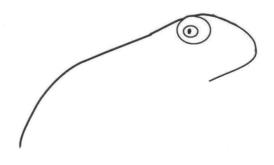

Add a front leg and foot.

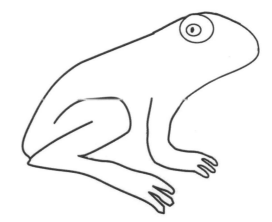

Add a back leg and foot.

Draw the second eye. Add a mouth and a nostril. Draw another front foot. Add a line for the frog's belly.

Color your frog.

Fantastic!

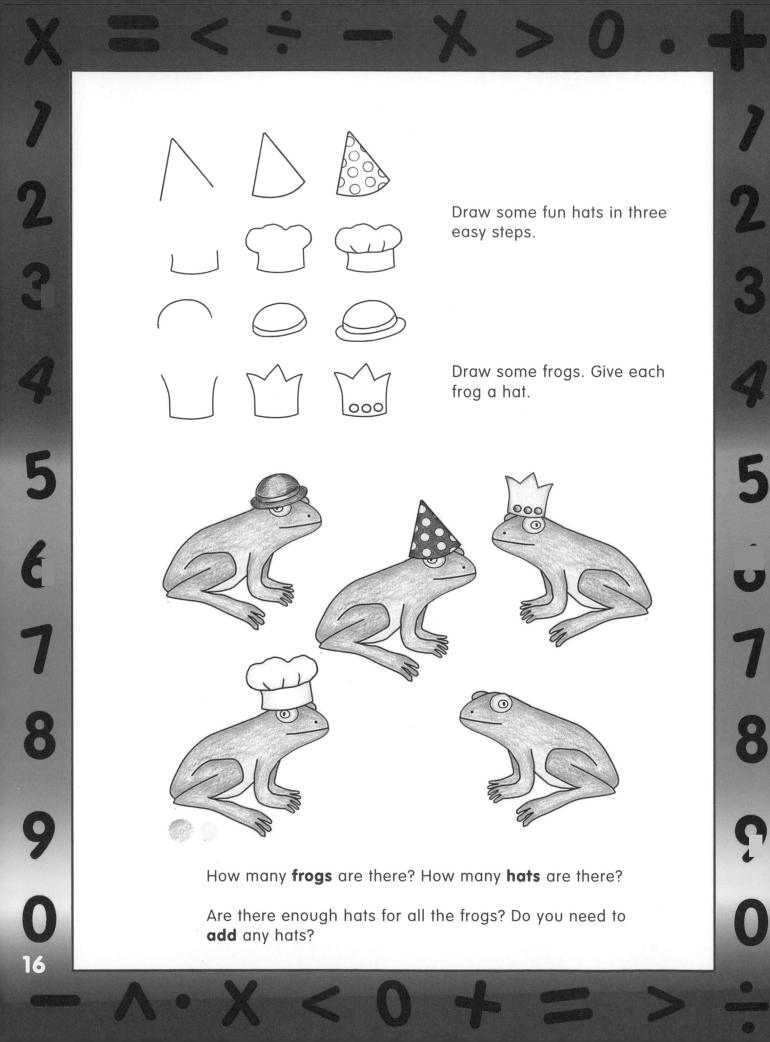

Draw some fun hats in three easy steps.

Draw some frogs. Give each frog a hat.

How many **frogs** are there? How many **hats** are there?

Are there enough hats for all the frogs? Do you need to **add** any hats?

Lesson Five: It All Adds Up

Counting by **groups** of two, three, and four.
Counting by **two**: 2 – 4 – 6 – 8 – 10....
Counting by t**hree**: 3 – 6 – 9 – 12 – 15....
Counting by **four**: 4 – 8 – 12 – 16 – 20....

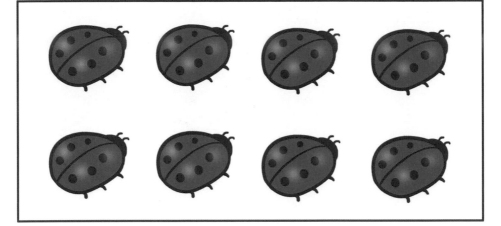

Look at the **red** ladybugs. Count them.
How many are there?
Now **count** by **twos**. Did the answer change?
How many **groups of two** are there?

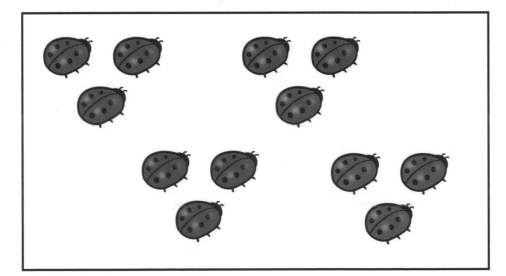

Count the ladybugs in the second box.
How many are there?
Now **count** by **threes**. Did the number change?
How many **groups of three** are there?

Let's draw a ladybug. Start with an egg shape. Draw a center line and a head.

Add dots. Draw feelers and three legs.

Color your ladybug.

Lovely Ladybug!

Draw a bunch of ladybugs and color them different colors.

How many different ways can you **count** the ladybugs you drew?

Lesson Six: Less and Less

Look at the **group** of four cars.

Hold your hand over **one** car. How many are left?

Hold your hand over **two** cars. How many are left?

Hold your hand over **three** cars. How many are left?

Let's draw a car.

Start with two circles. Draw two inner circles and a straight line.

Look at the top shape of the car. Draw the top shape of the car.

Add windows. Add headlights and tail lights.

Draw a door and handle. Add additional details you see.

Color your car.

Now that you know how to draw a car, let's make a **math sentence** using cars.

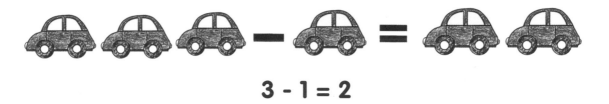

$$3 - 1 = 2$$

Three cars minus one car equals two cars.

or

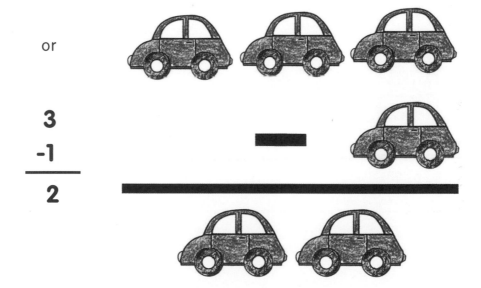

$$\begin{array}{r} 3 \\ -1 \\ \hline 2 \end{array}$$

Can you make a **math sentence** of your own?

Lesson Seven: More or Less

Count the **orange** cats.

Count the **purple** cats.

Which **group** has **more?**

Which group has **less?**

Let's draw a cat.

Start with a circle and a larger oval.
Notice the position of each shape.

Add two ears, two
eyes, a nose, and
a mouth. Draw a
tail.

Draw four legs.

Add an inner ear. Draw whiskers.
Add toes. Erase extra lines.

Color your cat.

Cute!

Draw two **groups** of cats.

Which group has **more** cats?

Which group has **less** cats?

Lesson Eight: We're Surrounded

There are **numbers** all around us in everyday life. Let's draw some things that have **numbers**.

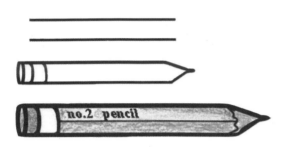

Let's start with a "Number Two" pencil. Draw two straight lines.

Add a point on one end and an eraser on the other.

Write "No. 2 Pencil" on the side and color your pencil.

Draw a clock. Start with a circle.

Draw an inner circle and add the **numbers** you see.

Draw a long and a short hand. Color your clock.

 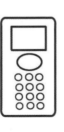 

Draw a cell phone. Start with a rectangle. Make the corners rounded.

Add a rectangle screen and circle buttons.

Put **numbers** in the circles and color the cell phone.

Draw a measuring cup. Start with a **trapezoid** shape.

Add a handle. Draw lines and **numbers** for measuring.

Finish your measuring cup.

Let's draw a clock radio. Start with a rectangle inside another rectangle.

Add two more rectangles. Divide one and add short lines for the radio dial.

Draw knobs on the sides. Add the clock **numbers**. Color your clock radio.

There are **numbers** on price tags we see everyday.

Draw a rectangle with a half circle on top. Add a circle for a hole. Erase extra lines.

Add the dollar price and lines for the store bar code. Color your price tag and add a string.

Look at the items with **numbers** below. Draw this kitchen scene.
Add some things from your own house that have **numbers**.

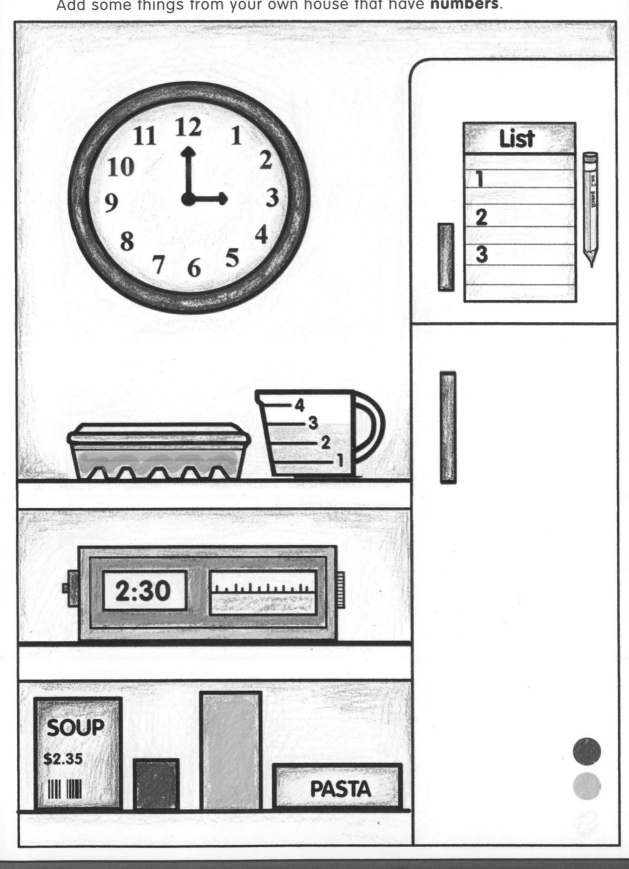

Lesson Nine: Shape Up!

Look carefully at the **shapes** below.

Which **shapes** have you been using in your drawings?

What **new shapes** do you see?

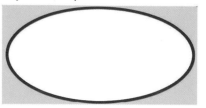

CIRCLE - SQUARE   OVAL - RECTANGLE

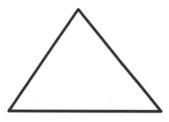
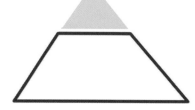

TRIANGLE   TRAPEZOID

PARALLELOGRAM

STAR

Try drawing the new **shapes**. The star might take more practice if you haven't drawn one before.

Let's use different **shapes** to draw a circus scene.

Starting at the top, draw a **circle** head and a **trapezoid** body for the clown. Add **rectangle** arms, **parallelogram** legs, and **triangle** feet.

Draw two **ovals** for the dog's head and body. Add two rectangle legs and a trapezoid stand.

Draw a triangle hat. Add two half circle**s** for ears and two circles for hands, Draw an **oval** for the clown's hoop.

Draw a trapezoid ear and a triangle tail for the dog. Add two more rectangle legs.

Draw circle eyes, part circle eyebrows, a circle nose, and a curved mouth. Add two circle buttons.

Give the dog a triangle and circle hat. Draw the dog's circle nose and eye. Add his curved mouth. Add **stars** to his stand.

Color your Circus **shape** scene.

Can you make up a **shape** picture of your own?

Lesson Ten: Quilt-y as Charged

Quilt patterns are made by sewing together small pieces of cloth that have been cut into **shapes**. This quilt pattern is called "Pinwheel".

Look at the quilt block below.

Name the **red shapes** that you see.

Name the **blue shapes** you see.

Name the **yellow shapes** you see.

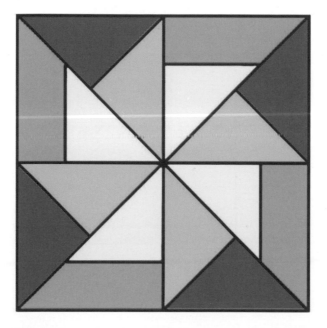

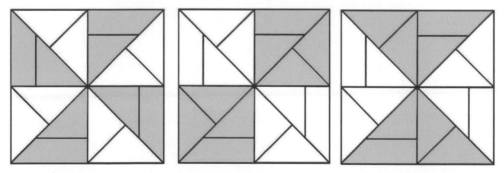

The shaded blue areas show big **shapes** that were created by combining several smaller **shapes**. Name the **blue shapes** that you see.

Let's make a quilt block with squares, rectangles, and triangles. This quilt block pattern is called "Crow's Feet".

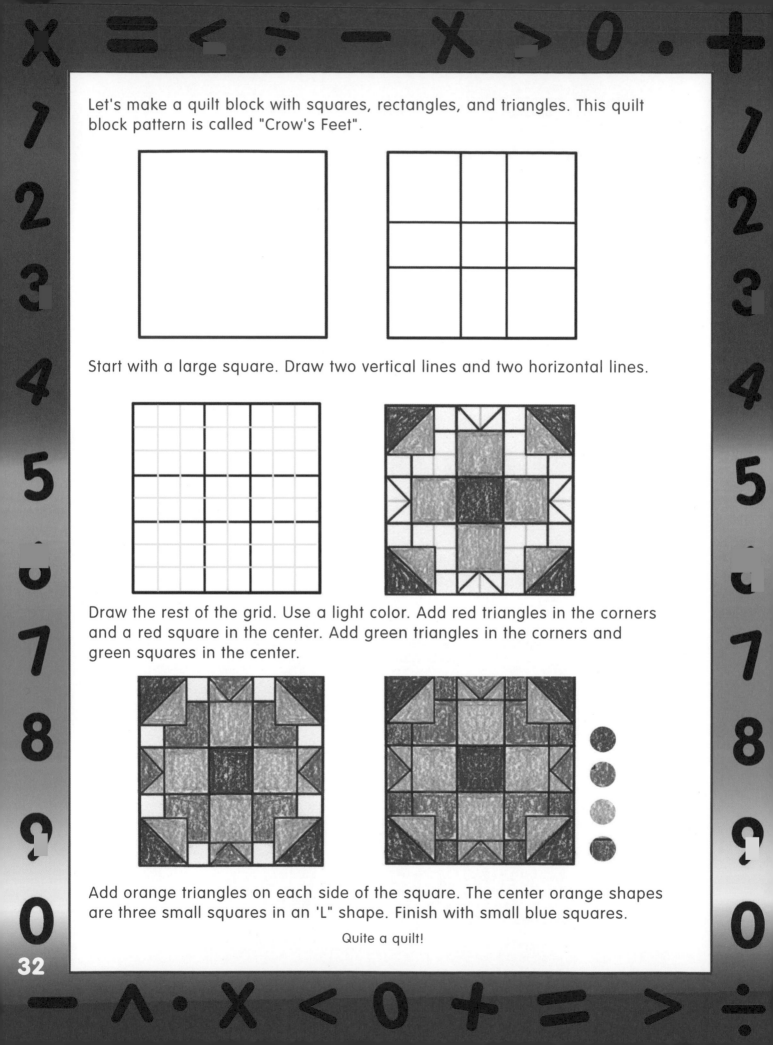

Start with a large square. Draw two vertical lines and two horizontal lines.

Draw the rest of the grid. Use a light color. Add red triangles in the corners and a red square in the center. Add green triangles in the corners and green squares in the center.

Add orange triangles on each side of the square. The center orange shapes are three small squares in an 'L" shape. Finish with small blue squares.

Quite a quilt!

Lesson Eleven: Mirror, Mirror

Some shapes and designs can be divided into two equal halves. Each half will be a mirror image of the other. We say these designs have **symmetry**. They are **symmetrical**.

The quilt blocks from the previous page are **symmetrical**.

A valentine heart is **symmetrical.**

Something as small as a snowflake or as large as the Eiffel Tower can be **symmetrical**.

Let's draw a **symmetrical** butterfly.

Start with the butterfly's body. Make two antennae.

Look at the wing shapes. Draw the upper wings. Add the lower wings.

Draw a design on the upper wings. Remember, whatever you put on one wing, you have to put on the other wing in reverse.

Draw a design on the lower wings.

Color your **symmetrical** butterfly.

Beautiful Butterfly!

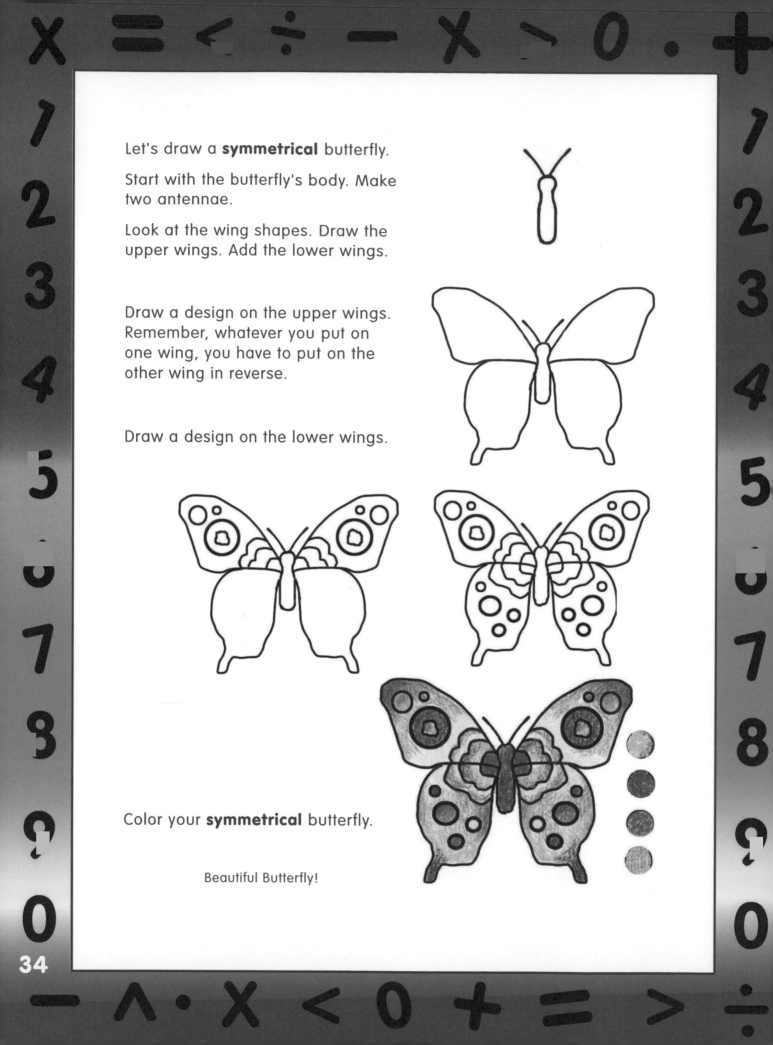

People are also **symmetrical**.

Draw an egg shape head. Add eyebrows, eyes, a nose, and a mouth. Draw two neck lines.

Draw the upper body.

Add arms and hands.

Draw legs and feet.

Add hair, a design on his shirt, and shoes.

Color your **symmetrical** person.

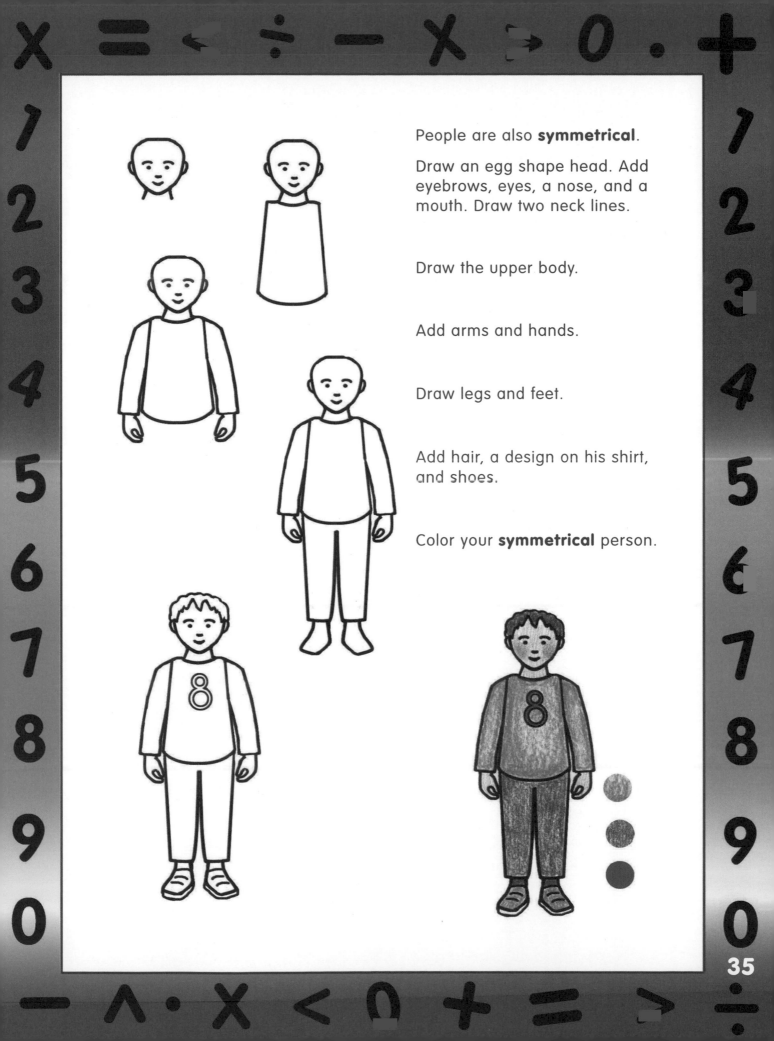

Lesson Twelve: I'm Beginning to See a Pattern

Look at the **patterns** below.

The first row is a color **pattern**:

Red. **Blue**. **R**ed. **Blue**. **R**ed. **Blue**.

What color would come **next** to continue the **pattern**?

The next row is a color and shape **pattern**:

Blue square. Green rectangle. Blue square. Green rectangle. Blue square. Green rectangle.

What would come **next**?

The next row is a color **pattern** and also a **pattern** of **groups**.

Three purple bugs. Two red bugs. Three purple bugs. Two red bugs. Three purple bugs.

What do you think will come **next**?

Let's draw a rabbit to use in rabbit **patterns**.

Draw a circle for the rabbit's head. Add two eyes and a nose. Add an oval body.

Add ears and front paws. Draw hind feet. Add some toes.

Make a rabbit **pattern** with **color**.

Make a rabbit **pattern** with **color** and **size**.

Make a rabbit **pattern** with **color, size,** and **groups**.

Are there other rabbit **patterns** you can make?

Lesson Thirteen: Match Maker

A **pattern** can be a design. Look at the mittens below.

What **patterns** do you see? Can you find the **matching** pairs? How many pairs did you find?

Look carefully at the **patterns** on the socks.

Does each sock have a **matching** sock?

Let's make a mouse and give her dresses with different **patterns**.

Draw a tear drop shape for her head. Add ears, two eyes, and a nose.

Draw her dress. It's shaped a bit like a piece of pie.

Add two arms. Draw two legs with little shoes.

Draw different **patterns** on her dresses with stripes, dots, and checks.

Can you make up a **pattern** of your own?

Nice mice!

Lesson Fourteen: It Takes All Sorts

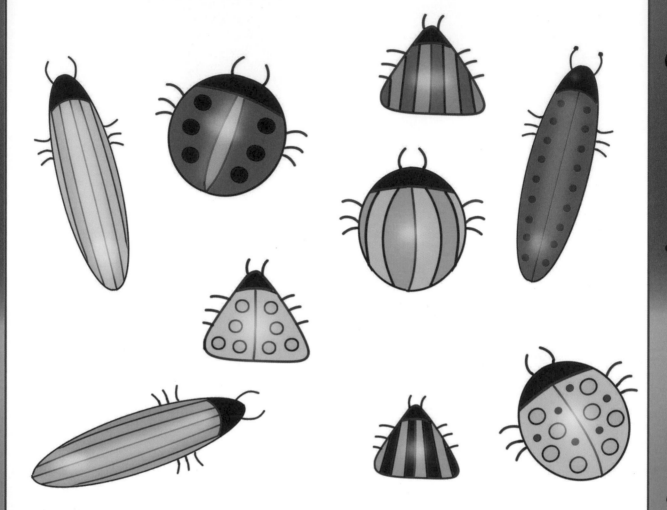

Look at the picture of bugs. There are all **sorts**.

How many **blue** bugs do you see?

How many **red** bugs do you see?

How many **green** bugs do you see?

How many **round** bugs do you see?

How many **long**, **thin** bugs do you see?

How many bugs are shaped liked a **triangle**?

How many bugs have **dots** and how many have **stripes**?

Things can be **sorted** in many different ways.

Let's draw some bugs in three easy steps.

Sort them according to **color**, **shape**, and **pattern.**

How many ways can you **sort** the bugs in your drawing?

Lesson Fifteen: Where Am I?

Which little alien is **under** his space ship?

Which little alien is **over** his space ship?

Which is **on** his space ship and which is **off** his space ship?

Which pictures show him **in** and **out** of his space ship?

Let's use these ideas to make a pet shop **picture**.

First, draw a mouse's head with a big ear. Add an eye, nose, and mouth.

Draw the second ear. Add the mouse's body.

Add a line for the inner ear. Draw the front and back paws. Add the tail.

Next, draw a parrot's head. Start with a circle. Add an eye and a curved beak.

Draw the parrot's curved body. Add a wing and a tail.

Add lines to the tail. Draw two feet.

Now, draw a turtle. Start with a half circle for the shell top. Add a curved line for the bottom. Draw a head and two feet.

Add an eye, a nose, and a mouth. Draw a tail.

Draw lines for the pattern of the turtle's shell. Draw lines on the turtle's neck. Add claws to the feet.

on

over

off

under

out

in

Make a pet shop **scene** using the ideas of **on** and **off**, **over** and **under**, and **in** and **out**. Label your picture.

Lesson Sixteen: What's Next?

Look at the three pairs of pictures below.

In each pair, the picture on the left comes first. The picture on the right comes **next**.

Pictures can show what comes **next.** In this way, you can tell a story with pictures.

Here are three sets of pictures that tell a story.

Let's draw a picture that **tells a story** of a bird's nest.

First draw a few pieces of straw for the nest.

Add more overlapping pieces of straw to shape the nest.

Draw an egg, sitting in the nest.

Draw the chick's head. Start with a circle. Add an eye and a beak.

Draw an oval body.

Add the lower beak and wings. Draw some fuzzy feathers on the chick.

Use the drawings to tell a little story.

The first picture is an egg in a nest.

The second picture shows the egg cracking open.

The third picture shows the chick in the nest.

If you mixed up the order of the pictures, it wouldn't make sense.

Each picture shows what comes **next**.

Can you draw a picture story of your own?

Lesson Seventeen: Share and Share Alike

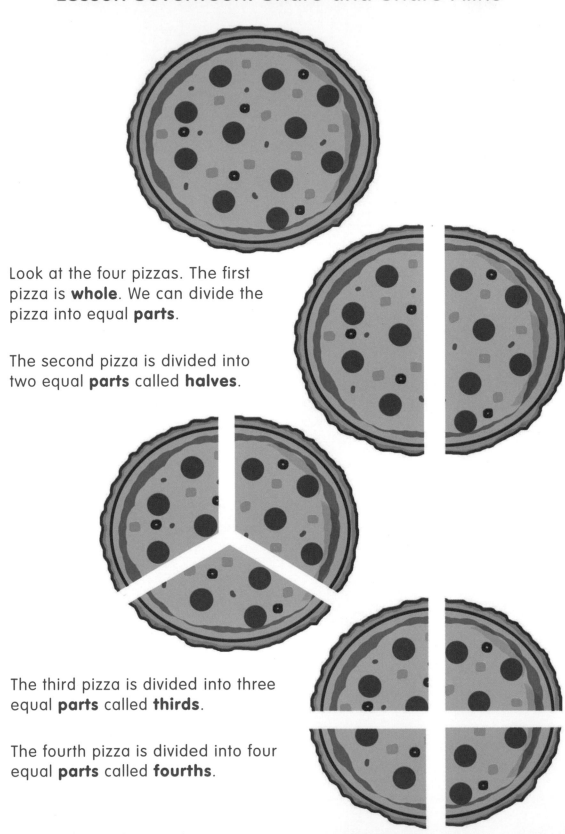

Look at the four pizzas. The first pizza is **whole**. We can divide the pizza into equal **parts**.

The second pizza is divided into two equal **parts** called **halves**.

The third pizza is divided into three equal **parts** called **thirds**.

The fourth pizza is divided into four equal **parts** called **fourths**.

Let's draw a pie and divide it into different **parts**.

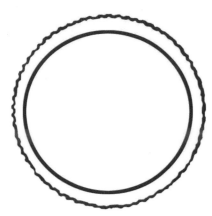

Start with a circle. Add the outer rim of the pie.

Draw a few steam vents on top of the pie. Add some nice fork marks around the rim. Color your **whole** pie.

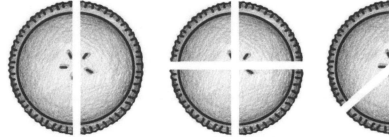

Draw three pies. Cut one into two **halves**.

Cut one into four **fourths**.

Cut one into three **thirds**.

M-M-M-M PIE! (My pie is blueberry. What's yours?)

Let's draw a puppy.

Start with a circle for the head. Add two eyes, a nose, and a mouth. Draw ears.

Add the body. Draw two front paws.

Draw two back legs and paws.

Color your puppy.

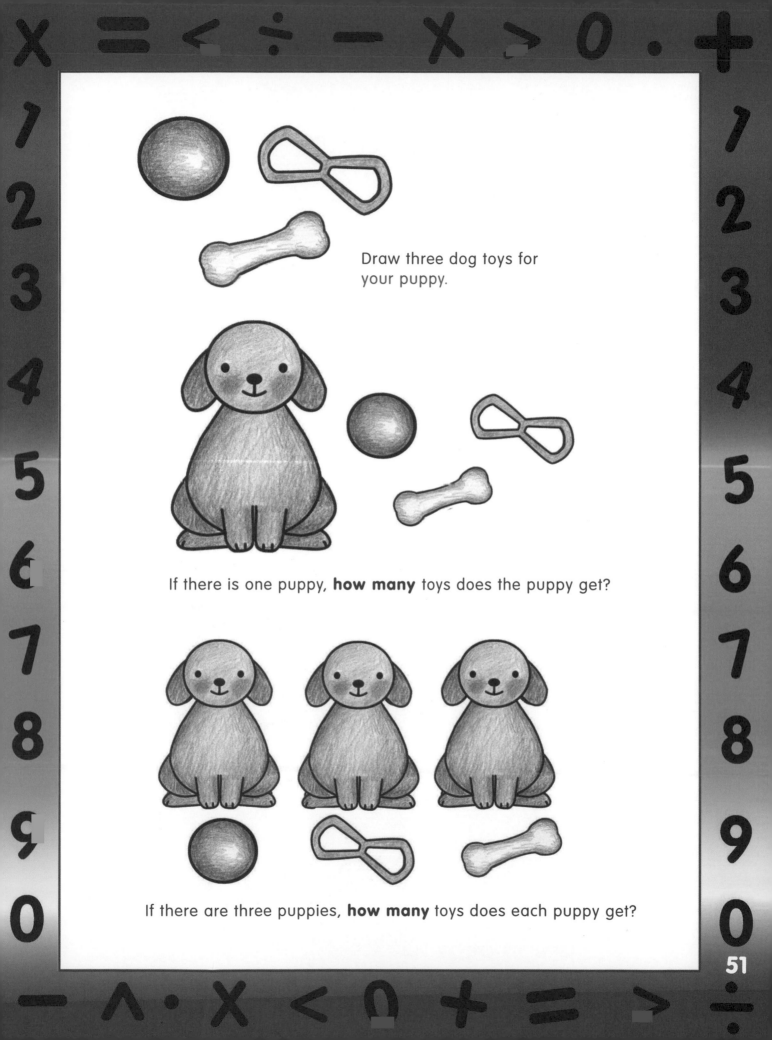

Draw three dog toys for your puppy.

If there is one puppy, **how many** toys does the puppy get?

If there are three puppies, **how many** toys does each puppy get?

Let's draw a cat.

Start with a circle. Add two
eyes, a nose, and a
mouth.

Draw ears and whiskers.
Add the cat's body.

Draw front paws. Draw two
back legs and paws. Add
a tail.

Color your cat.

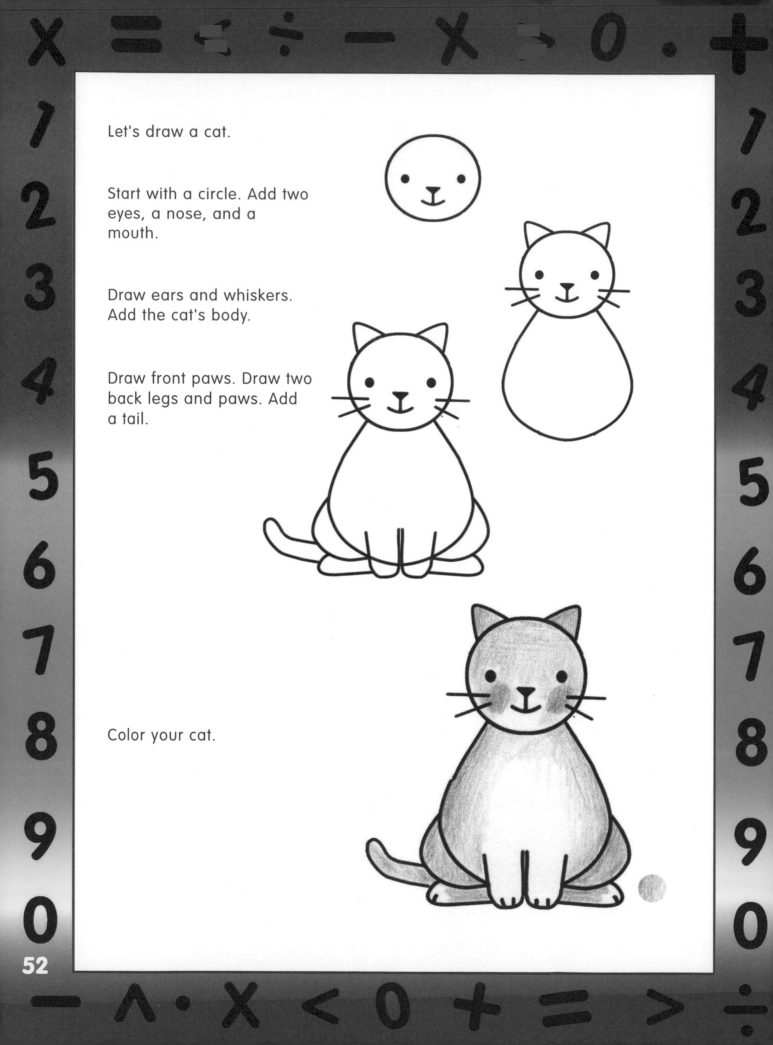

Let's draw six toy mice. If there is one cat, **how many** mice would the cat get?

If there were three cats, **how many** mice would each cat get?

Lesson Eighteen: Information Please

Look at the three robots. They are all **different**.

Point to the robot that has a yellow face, blue arms, and red feet.

Point to the robot that has blue legs, red feet, a green body, and a red face.

Point to the robot that has blue arms, a yellow face, and red legs.

You are using **information** about the robots to pick the right one.

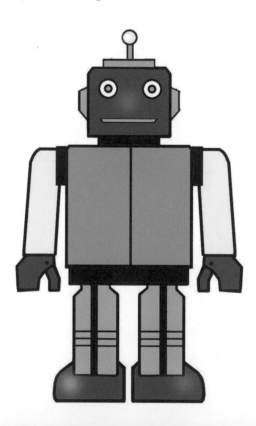

Let's draw a robot.

Start with a small square and a big square. Connect the squares with two lines. Draw two eyes and a mouth. Add an antenna on top of the robot's head.

Add ear pieces. Draw two arms. Divide the large square with a vertical line. Add a black rectangle under the square.

Draw legs and hands.

Look at the design on the legs. Draw this and add shoes.

Using the four colors and the **information** you have about the robots on page 54, make your robot **different**.

Rockin' Robot!

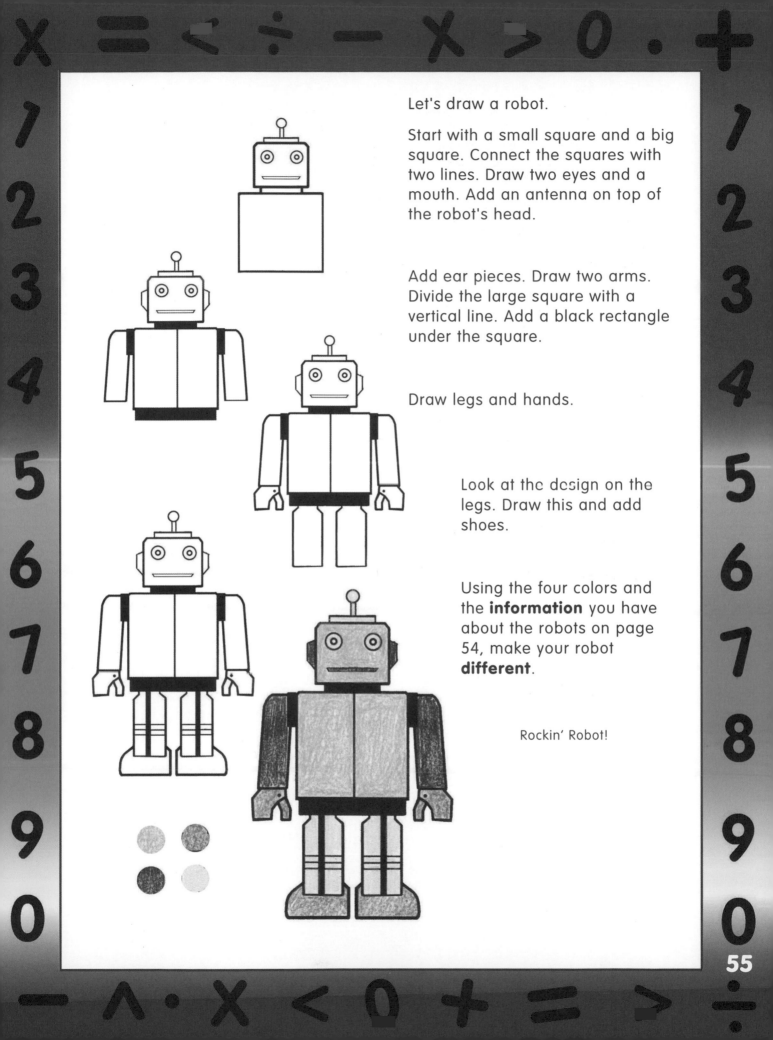

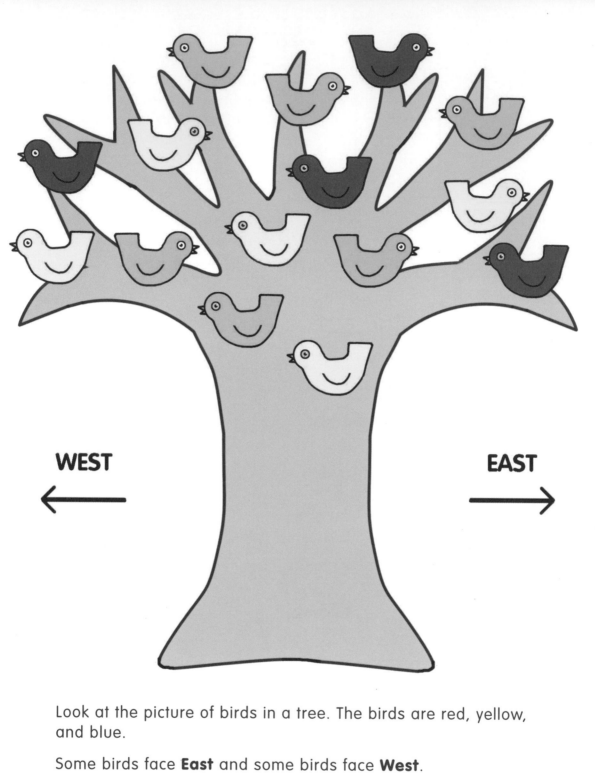

WEST ←

EAST →

Look at the picture of birds in a tree. The birds are red, yellow, and blue.

Some birds face **East** and some birds face **West**.

Let's use **information** about the birds to create a **graph**.

Start with a square. Divide it into three vertical columns. Label the columns

RED, YELLOW, and BLUE.

Divide the columns into six spaces. Each box represents one bird.

Starting at the bottom, label the columns 1 through 6.

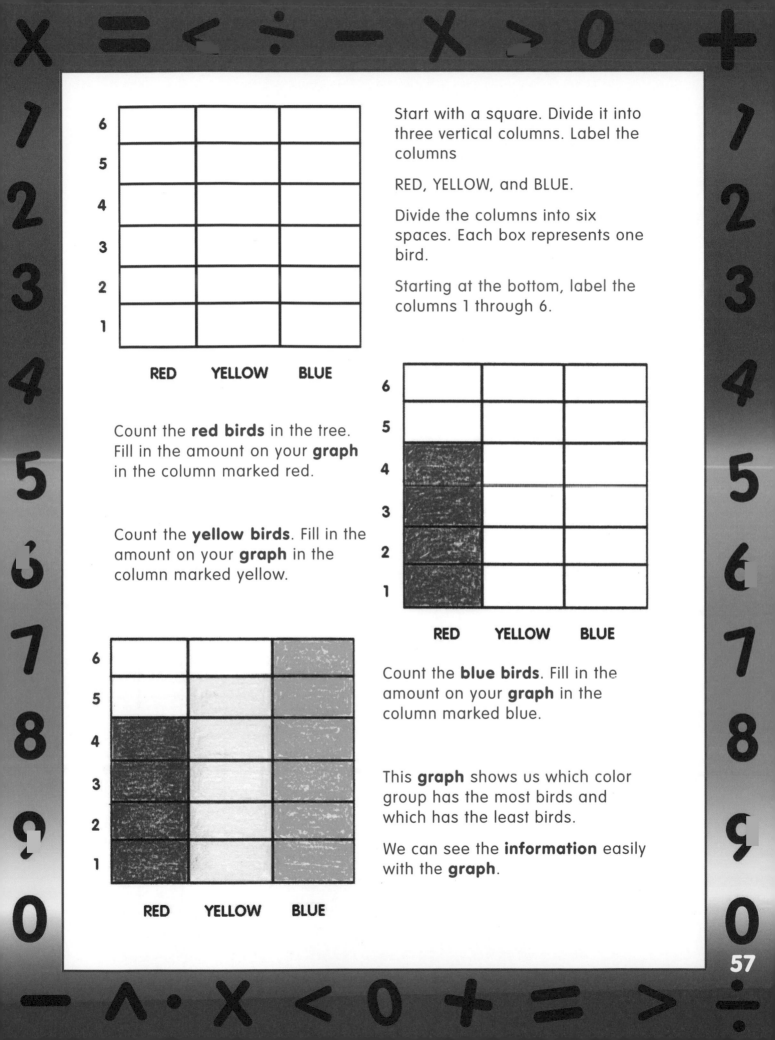

RED   YELLOW   BLUE

Count the **red birds** in the tree. Fill in the amount on your **graph** in the column marked red.

Count the **yellow birds**. Fill in the amount on your **graph** in the column marked yellow.

RED   YELLOW   BLUE

Count the **blue birds**. Fill in the amount on your **graph** in the column marked blue.

This **graph** shows us which color group has the most birds and which has the least birds.

We can see the **information** easily with the **graph**.

RED   YELLOW   BLUE

Let's make another **graph** using the same picture.

Draw a square. Divide it into six vertical columns. Then divide it into six horizontal columns. Each square equals one bird.

Look at the labels on each column. Label your **graph** the same way.

RED: LOOKS EAST

RED: LOOKS WEST

YELLOW: LOOKS EAST

YELLOW: LOOKS WEST

BLUE: LOOKS EAST

BLUE LOOKS WEST

1   2   3   4   5   6

Count the **red birds looking East**. Fill in that row.

Count the **red birds looking West**. Fill in that row.

Do the same for each of the rows.

The **graph** you made gives you **information** about the picture.

The **information** can also be called **data**.

What does it tell you about the groups of birds in the picture?

RED: LOOKS EAST

RED: LOOKS WEST

YELLOW: LOOKS EAST

YELLOW: LOOKS WEST

BLUE: LOOKS EAST

BLUE LOOKS WEST

1   2   3   4   5   6

Lesson Nineteen: Combination Plate

Look at the two stars. One is red and one is green.

We can make two **combinations**: **red/green** and **green/red**.

What if we increase the amount of stars? Now there are three stars: one red, one green, and one yellow. How many **combinations** can we make? Count the **combinations**.

Let's try four stars: **red**, **green**, **yellow**, and **blue**.

How many **combinations** are there? **Count** the **combinations**.

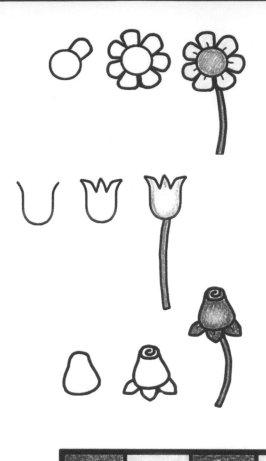

Let's make a picture using different **combinations** of flowers.

Draw three flowers: a daisy, a tulip, and a rose. Draw each flower in three steps.

Draw a flower shop window with all the possible **combinations** of the three flowers.

How many **combinations** did you make? Check page 59 to see how many **combinations** were made with three stars. Does it match?

Lesson Twenty: Ready, Set, Draw!

Here is a math and drawing game.

Take eighteen small pieces of paper. On six pieces of paper, write the numbers one through six.

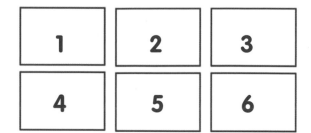

On six pieces of paper, write six different colors.

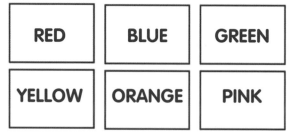

On six pieces of paper, write the name of six different objects.

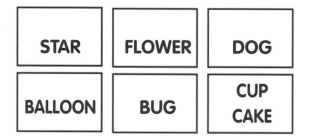

Turn the papers over. Each player will pick six sets. A number, a color, and an object will make one set. Here are the six sets I picked:

5 green stars
4 pink cupcakes
3 yellow flowers
2 red bugs
1 orange dog
6 blue balloons

You can see on the next page how I made my drawing with these sets.

Have each player take a big piece of paper and make a drawing using all six of the sets they picked. Try dividing into teams or using a timer.

Have fun!

Index